The Wiersbe

BIBLE STUDY SERIES

1 JOHN

The Wiersbe
BIBLE STUDY SERIES

Turning

from

Hypocrisy

to Truth

DAVID C COOK

transforming lives together

THE WIERSBE BIBLE STUDY SERIES: 1 JOHN
Published by David C Cook
4050 Lee Vance Drive
Colorado Springs, CO 80918 U.S.A.

Integrity Music Limited, a Division of David C Cook
Brighton, East Sussex BN1 2RE, England

The graphic circle C logo is a registered trademark of David C Cook.

All Scripture quotations in this study are taken from the Holy Bible, New
International Version®, NIV®. Copyright © 1973, 1978, 1984 by Biblica, Inc™. Used
by permission of Zondervan. All rights reserved worldwide. www.zondervan.com.

In the *Be Real* excerpts, unless otherwise noted, all Scripture quotations are taken
from the King James Version of the Bible. (Public Domain.) Scripture quotations
marked NASB are taken from the *New American Standard Bible,* © Copyright 1960,
1995 by The Lockman Foundation. Used by permission; and PH are taken from J. B.
Phillips: *The New Testament in Modern English,* revised editions © J. B. Phillips, 1958,
1960, 1972, permission of Macmillan Publishing Co. and Collins Publishers.

All excerpts taken from *Be Real,* second edition, published by David C Cook
in 2009 © 1972 Warren W. Wiersbe, ISBN 978-1-4347-6744-8.

ISBN 978-0-7814-0456-3
eISBN 978-1-4347-0405-4

© 2011 Warren W. Wiersbe

The Team: Steve Parolini, Karen Lee-Thorp,
Amy Kiechlin Konyndyk, Sarah Schultz, Jack Campbell, Karen Athen
Series Cover Design: John Hamilton Design
Cover Photo: Veer DVP4972337

Printed in the United States of America
First Edition 2011

7 8 9 10 11 12 13 14 15 16

032119

Contents

Introduction to 1 John

The Real Life

"Once upon a time …" Remember how exciting those words used to be? They were the open door into an exciting make-believe dreamworld that helped you forget all the problems of childhood.

Then—*pow!* You turned a corner one day, and "Once upon a time" became kid stuff. You discovered that life is a battleground, not a playground, and fairy tales were no longer meaningful. You wanted something real. The search for something real is not new. It has been going on since the beginning of history. People have looked for reality and satisfaction in wealth, thrills, conquest, power, learning, and religion.

There is nothing really wrong with these experiences, except that by themselves they never really satisfy. Wanting something real and finding something real are two different things. Like a child eating cotton candy at the circus, many people who expect to bite into something real end up with a mouthful of nothing. They waste priceless years on empty substitutes for reality.

This is where the apostle John's first epistle comes in. Written centuries ago, this letter deals with a theme that is forever up-to-date: the life that is real.

Revealed!

As you read John's letter, you will discover that he enjoyed using certain words and that the word *manifest* is one of them. "For the life was manifested," he said (1 John 1:2 KJV). This life was not hidden so that we have to search for it and find it. No, it was manifested—revealed openly! If you were God, how would you go about revealing yourself to people? How could you tell them about, and give them, the kind of life you wanted them to enjoy?

God has revealed Himself in creation (Rom. 1:20), but creation alone could never tell us the story of God's love. God has also revealed Himself much more fully in His Word, the Bible. But God's final and most complete revelation is in His Son, Jesus Christ. Jesus said, "He that hath seen me hath seen the Father" (John 14:9 KJV).

Because Jesus is God's revelation of Himself, He has a very special name: "The Word of life" (1 John 1:1 KJV). This same title opens John's gospel: "In the beginning was the Word, and the Word was with God, and the Word was God" (John 1:1 KJV). Why does Jesus Christ have this name? Because Christ is to us what our words are to others. Our words reveal to others just what we think and how we feel. Christ reveals to us the mind and heart of God. He is the living means of communication between God and humankind. To know Jesus Christ is to know God! And to know God is to be real!

—Warren W. Wiersbe

How to Use This Study

This study is designed for both individual and small-group use. We've divided it into eight lessons—each references one or more chapters in Warren W. Wiersbe's commentary *Be Real* (second edition, David C Cook, 2009). While reading *Be Real* is not a prerequisite for going through this study, the additional insights and background Wiersbe offers can greatly enhance your study experience.

The **Getting Started** questions at the beginning of each lesson offer you an opportunity to record your first thoughts and reactions to the study text. This is an important step in the study process as those "first impressions" often include clues about what it is your heart is longing to discover.

The bulk of the study is found in the **Going Deeper** questions. These dive into the Bible text and, along with helpful excerpts from Wiersbe's commentary, help you examine not only the original context and meaning of the verses but also modern application.

Looking Inward narrows the focus down to your personal story. These intimate questions can be a bit uncomfortable at times, but don't shy away from honesty here. This is where you are asked to stand before the mirror of God's Word and look closely at what you see. It's the place to take a good look at yourself in light of the lesson and search for ways in which you can grow in faith.

Going Forward is the place where you can commit to paper those things you want or need to do in order to better live out the discoveries you made in the Looking Inward section. Don't skip or skim through this. Take the time to really consider what practical steps you might take to move closer to Christ. Then share your thoughts with a trusted friend who can act as an encourager and accountability partner.

Finally, there is a brief **Seeking Help** section to close the lesson. This is a reminder for you to invite God into your spiritual-growth process. If you choose to write out a prayer in this section, come back to it as you work through the lesson and continue to seek the Holy Spirit's guidance as you discover God's will for your life.

Tips for Small Groups

A small group is a dynamic thing. One week it might seem like a group of close-knit friends. The next it might seem more like a group of uncomfortable strangers. A small-group leader's role is to read these subtle changes and adjust the tone of the discussion accordingly.

Small groups need to be safe places for people to talk openly. It is through shared wrestling with difficult life issues that some of the greatest personal growth is discovered. But in order for the group to feel safe, participants need to know it's okay *not* to share sometimes. Always invite honest disclosure, but never force someone to speak if he or she isn't comfortable doing so. (A savvy leader will follow up later with a group member who isn't comfortable sharing in a group setting to see if a one-on-one discussion is more appropriate.)

Have volunteers take turns reading excerpts from Scripture or from the commentary. The more each person is involved even in the mundane tasks, the more they'll feel comfortable opening up in more meaningful ways.

The leader should watch the clock and keep the discussion moving. Sometimes there may be more Going Deeper questions than your group can cover in your available time. If you've had a fruitful discussion, it's okay to move on without finishing everything. And if you think the group is getting bogged down on a question or has taken off on a tangent, you can simply say, "Let's go on to question 5." Be sure to save at least ten to fifteen minutes for the Going Forward questions.

Finally, soak your group meetings in prayer—before you begin, during as needed, and always at the end of your time together.

Real
(1 JOHN 1:1—2:6)

Before you begin …
- *Pray for the Holy Spirit to reveal truth and wisdom as you go through this lesson.*
- *Read 1 John 1:1—2:6. This lesson references chapters 1 and 2 in* Be Real. *It will be helpful for you to have your Bible and a copy of the commentary available as you work through this lesson.*

Getting Started

From the Commentary

Read the first four verses of John's letter again, and you will notice that the apostle had a personal encounter with Jesus Christ. His was no secondhand "religious experience" inherited from somebody else or discovered in a book! No, John knew Jesus Christ face-to-face. He and the other apostles heard Jesus speak. They watched Him as He lived with them. In fact, they studied Him carefully, and even touched His body. They knew that

Jesus was real—not a phantom, not a vision, but God in human corporeal form.

—*Be Real,* page 22

1. How does the fact that the author of 1 John had firsthand knowledge of Jesus influence his message? How, if at all, does it affect the way you read 1 John?

More to Consider: Did John have an "advantage" in his faith because of his physical nearness to Jesus? Why or why not?

2. Choose one verse or phrase from 1 John 1:1—2:6 that stands out to you. This could be something you're intrigued by, something that makes you uncomfortable, something that puzzles you, something that resonates with you, or just something you want to examine further. Write that here.

Going Deeper

From the Commentary

> John wrote this letter to share Christ with us. As you read it, you will discover that John had in mind five purposes for sharing.
>
> (1) That we may have fellowship (1:3).
>
> (2) That we may have joy (1:4).
>
> (3) That we may not sin (2:1).
>
> (4) That we may not be deceived (2:26).
>
> (5) That we may know we are saved (5:13).
>
> —*Be Real,* pages 26–29

3. As you consider the five purposes for John's letter noted above, what do they say about the intended audience for the letter? How was John's letter appropriate for the early Christians? What makes his message timeless?

From the Commentary

Every form of life has its enemies. Insects have to watch out for hungry birds, and birds must keep an eye on hungry cats and dogs. Even human beings have to dodge automobiles and fight off germs.

The life that is real also has an enemy, and we read about it in 1 John 1:5—2:6. This enemy is sin. Nine times in these verses John mentioned sin, so the subject is obviously not unimportant. John illustrated his theme by using the contrast between light and darkness: God is light; sin is darkness.

But there is another contrast here too—the contrast between saying and doing. Four times John wrote, "If we say" or "He that saith" (1 John 1:6, 8, 10; 2:4). It is clear that our Christian life is to amount to more than mere "talk"; we must also "walk," or live, what we believe. If we are in fellowship with God (if we are "walking in the light"), our lives will back up what our lips are saying. But if we are living in sin ("walking in darkness"), then our lives will contradict what our lips are saying, making us hypocrites.

—Be Real, page 35

4. Circle every time John mentioned sin. What is significant about the context of these mentions? Why did John include "if ... then" statements in this section? What does this teach us about the words we say? About the claims we make as believers?

From Today's World

In the 1960s, Episcopalian priest Joseph Fletcher's book *Situation Ethics* popularized an ethical theory of Christian moral relativism. In his book, Fletcher set up the idea that love is the ultimate law and the only absolute and that all other laws are guidelines on how to achieve love; therefore, they can be broken if doing so would result in more love. Fletcher was a pioneer in the field of bioethics, which explores the intersection of ethics and medicine in such diverse areas as abortion, euthanasia, organ donation, and the right to refuse medical treatment. This topic has become particularly significant in recent years and continues to be controversial in religious and nonreligious circles.

5. First John is a book all about love, but it doesn't shy away from identifying sin as an obstacle to love. How do Joseph Fletcher's situational ethics line up with John's message? Where do the two diverge? What are the problems with situational ethics? How did John directly (and indirectly) address these in 1 John?

From the Commentary

"God is light, and in him is no darkness at all" (1 John 1:5). When we were saved, God called us out of darkness into His light (1 Peter 2:9). We are children of light (1 Thess. 5:5). Those who do wrong hate light (John 3:19–21). When light shines in on us, it reveals our true nature (Eph. 5:8–13).

Light produces life and growth and beauty, but sin is darkness; and darkness and light cannot exist in the same place. If we are walking in the light, the darkness has to go. If we are holding to sin, then the light goes. There is no middle ground, no vague "gray" area, where sin is concerned.

—*Be Real,* page 37

6. Review 1 John 1:5–6, 8, 10; 2:4. What do these verses reveal about sin? How do Christians try to cover up their sins? What motivates Christians to cover up their sins? What is John's answer to this?

From the Commentary

At this point we must discuss an extremely important factor in our experience of the life that is real. That factor is honesty. We must be honest with ourselves, honest with others, and honest with God. Our passage describes a believer who is living a dishonest life: He is a phony. He is playing a role and acting a part, but is not living a genuine life. He is insincere.

—*Be Real,* page 38

7. Read 1 John 1:5–10. Summarize this passage. What kinds of losses does the person who makes these false claims incur? How common is this sort of person in today's world? What is the lure of living a false life? What are the dangers of living a life that isn't genuine?

From the Commentary

John gave two interesting titles to Jesus Christ: "advocate" and "propitiation" (1 John 2:1–2). It's important that we understand these two titles because they stand for two ministries that only the Lord Himself performs.

Let's begin with "propitiation." If you look this word up in the dictionary, you may get the wrong idea of its meaning. The dictionary tells us that "to propitiate" means "to appease someone who is angry." If you apply this to

Christ, you get the horrible picture of an angry God, about to destroy the world, and a loving Savior giving Himself to appease the irate God—and this is not the Bible picture of salvation! Certainly God is angry at sin; after all, He is infinitely holy. But the Bible reassures us that "God so loved [not hated] the world" (John 3:16).

No, the word *propitiation* does not mean the appeasing of an angry God. Rather, it means the satisfying of God's holy law. "God is light" (1 John 1:5), and therefore He cannot close His eyes to sin. But "God is love" (4:8) too and wants to save sinners.

—*Be Real,* pages 40–41

8. What stands out to you about the way John described Jesus in this section? How can a holy God uphold justice and still forgive?

More to Consider: The word John uses for advocate *in this section is the very same word Jesus used when He was talking about the coming of the Holy Spirit (John 14:16, 26; 15:26). In this context, what does* advocate *mean? What does this shared term teach us about the relationship between Jesus and the Holy Spirit?*

From the Commentary

When we confess our sins, God promises to forgive us (1 John 1:9). But this promise is not a "magic rabbit's foot" that makes it easy for us to disobey God!

"I went out and sinned," a student told his campus chaplain, "because I knew I could come back and ask God to forgive me."

"On what basis can God forgive you?" the chaplain asked, pointing to 1 John 1:9.

"God is faithful and just," the boy replied.

"Those two words should have kept you out of sin," the chaplain said. "Do you know what it cost God to forgive your sins?"

The boy hung his head. "Jesus had to die for me."

Then the chaplain zeroed in. "That's right—forgiveness isn't some cheap sideshow trick God performs. God is faithful to His promise, and God is just, because Christ died for your sins and paid the penalty for you. Now, the next time you plan to sin, remember that you are going to sin against a faithful, loving God!"

The blood of Jesus Christ, shed on the cross, delivers us

from the guilt of sin and gives us right standing ("justification") before God. God is able to forgive because Jesus' death has satisfied His holy law.

But God is also interested in cleansing a sinner inwardly. David prayed, "Create in me a clean heart, O God" (Ps. 51:10). When our confession is sincere, God does a cleansing work (1 John 1:9) in our hearts by His Spirit and through His Word (John 15:3).

—*Be Real,* page 43

9. Here is another "if … then" statement from John (1 John 1:9). What is our responsibility in this equation? What does that look like in practice? What is the difference between the judicial and personal aspects of God's forgiveness? How should each affect a believer's daily living?

From the Commentary

John makes it clear that Christians do not have to sin. "I am writing these things to you that you may not sin" (1 John 2:1 NASB).

The secret of victory over sin is found in the phrase "walk in the light" (1 John 1:7).

To walk in the light means to be open and honest, to be sincere. Paul prayed that his friends might "be sincere and without offense" (Phil. 1:10). The word *sincere* comes from two Latin words, *sine* and *cera*, which mean "without wax." It seems that in Roman days, some sculptors covered up their mistakes by filling the defects in their marble statues with wax, which was not readily visible—until the statue had been exposed to the hot sun awhile. But more dependable sculptors made certain that their customers knew that the statues they sold were *sine cera*—without wax.

It is unfortunate that churches and Bible classes have been invaded by insincere people, people whose lives cannot stand to be tested by God's light. "God is light," and when we walk in the light, there is nothing we can hide. It is refreshing to meet a Christian who is open and sincere and is not trying to masquerade!

—*Be Real,* page 44

10. What does it mean, practically speaking, to "walk in the light"? What does the light reveal? What should our response be to that revelation?

Looking Inward

Take a moment to reflect on all that you've explored thus far in this study of 1 John. Review your notes and answers and think about how each of these things matters in your life today.

Tips for Small Groups: To get the most out of this section, form pairs or trios and have group members take turns answering these questions. Be honest and as open as you can in this discussion, but most of all, be encouraging and supportive of others. Be sensitive to those who are going through particularly difficult times and don't press for people to speak if they're uncomfortable doing so.

11. How might your faith be different if you'd spent time with Jesus while He was on earth, as did the author of 1 John? How does the fact that you don't have that firsthand experience influence your faith today?

12. How successful are you at doing what you say when it comes to your faith? What are some ways you're walking in the light? What are some ways you're still stumbling in the darkness? How can you invite more light into your life?

13. Are you good at being honest with yourself? Why or why not? What are the obstacles that keep you from living a genuine life? How can you overcome those obstacles?

Going Forward

14. Think of one or two things you have learned that you'd like to work on in the coming week. Remember that this is all about quality, not quantity. It's better to work on one specific area of life and do it well than to work on many and do poorly (or to be so overwhelmed that you simply don't try).

Do you want to discover how to be more loving? Do you want to learn how to be more genuine in your faith? Be specific. Go back through 1 John 1:1—2:6 and put a star next to the phrase or verse that is most encouraging to you. Consider memorizing this verse.

Real-Life Application Ideas: What would it look like in practical terms to "walk in the light" this coming week? Take inventory of your plans and priorities and think about ways you can love others with a genuine love at work, home, or elsewhere. This might include being patient with the checkout person at the grocery store or offering a kind word to a friend who's suffering. Look for little ways to express love to others. Then take that practice on into the next week. And the next. And the next.

Seeking Help

15. Write a prayer below (or simply pray one in silence), inviting God to work on your mind and heart in those areas you've noted above. Be honest about your desires and fears.

Notes for Small Groups:

- *Look for ways to put into practice the things you wrote in the Going Forward section. Talk with other group members about your ideas and commit to being accountable to one another.*

- *During the coming week, ask the Holy Spirit to continue to reveal truth to you from what you've read and studied.*

- *Before you start the next lesson, read 1 John 2:7–11. For more in-depth lesson preparation, read chapter 3, "Something Old, Something New," in* Be Real.

⊞Love, Life, Light
(1 JOHN 2:7–11)

Before you begin …
- *Pray for the Holy Spirit to reveal truth and wisdom as you go through this lesson.*
- *Read 1 John 2:7–11. This lesson references chapter 3 in* Be Real. *It will be helpful for you to have your Bible and a copy of the commentary available as you work through this lesson.*

Getting Started

From the Commentary

I just *love* that hat!"

"Man, I really *love* the old-fashioned kind of baked beans!"

"But, Mom, don't you realize that Tom and I *love* each other?"

Words, like coins, can be in circulation for such a long time that they start wearing out. Unfortunately, the word *love* is losing its value and is being used to cover a multitude of sins.

It is really difficult to understand how a man can use the same word to express his love for his wife as he uses to tell how he feels about baked beans! When words are used that carelessly, they really mean little or nothing at all. Like the dollar, they have been devalued.

As John described the life that is real, he used three words repeatedly: life, love, and light. In fact, he devoted three sections of his letter to the subject of Christian love. He explained that *love, life,* and *light* belong together. Read these three sections (1 John 2:7–11; 3:10–24; 4:7–21) without the intervening verses, and you will see that love, life, and light must not be separated.

—*Be Real,* page 51

1. What are some ways the word *love* has been devalued? What are other words with positive meanings that have been devalued? Why does this happen? How can we recapture the true meaning of words like *love* in a culture where words tend to lose their meanings so quickly?

2. Choose one verse or phrase from 1 John 2:7–11 that stands out to you. This could be something you're intrigued by, something that makes you uncomfortable, something that puzzles you, something that resonates with you, or just something you want to examine further. Write that here.

Going Deeper

From the Commentary

> John not only wrote about love but also practiced it. One of his favorite names for his readers was "Beloved." He felt love for them. John is known as the "apostle of love" because in his gospel and his epistles he gives such prominence to this subject. However, John was not always the apostle of love. At one time Jesus gave John and his brother James, both of whom had hot tempers, the nickname "Boanerges" (Mark 3:17), which means "sons of thunder." On another occasion these two brothers wanted to call down fire from heaven to destroy a village (Luke 9:51–56).
>
> *—Be Real,* page 52

3. What does the word *beloved* imply that *friend* does not? What does the picture of John in Mark 3:17 teach us about the power of love to change a person's behavior or character? Is it possible to always be a disciple of love? Why or why not?

More to Consider: When we read in 1 John about love, the Greek word used is agape *(AH-ga-pay), the word for God's love toward people, a Christian's love for other Christians, and God's love for His church (Eph. 5:22–33). How is this definition of love unique?*

From the Commentary

The amazing thing is that Christian love is both old and new (1 John 2:7–8). This seems to be a contradiction. Love itself, of course, is not new, nor is the commandment—that men love God and one another—a new thing. Jesus Himself combined two Old Testament commandments, Deuteronomy 6:5 and Leviticus 19:18, and said (Mark 12:28–34) that these two commandments summarize all the law and the prophets. Loving God and loving one's neighbor were old, familiar responsibilities before Jesus ever came to earth.

—*Be Real,* page 53

4. Read 1 John 2:8. In what sense is loving one another a new commandment? How did John emphasize this sense of newness?

From the Commentary

In 1 John 2:3–6, John had been talking about "the commandments" in general, but now he narrowed his focus down to one single commandment. In the Old Testament, the command that God's people love one another was only one of many, but now this old commandment is lifted out and given a place of preeminence.…

It's doubtful that the fear of the law is often the motive behind earning a living or caring for one's children. Parents fulfill their responsibilities (even if grudgingly on occasion) because they love each other and their children. To them, doing the right thing is not a matter of law—it's a matter of love.

The commandment "Love one another" is the fulfillment of God's law in the same way. When you love people, you do not lie about them or steal from them. You have no desire to kill them. Love for God and love for others motivates a person to obey God's commandments without even thinking about them! When a person acts out of Christian love he obeys God and serves others—not because of fear, but because of his love.

—*Be Real,* pages 53–54

5. How does the commandment to "love one another" stand apart from any other commandment? What circumstances in the early church might have prompted John to focus on this commandment above all others? How is the truth of this commandment seen in Jesus' followers? What is the "true light" that is already shining (v. 8)?

More to Consider: The best description of Christian love is found in 1 Corinthians 13. Read this chapter. How does this definition of love complement the teaching in 1 John?

From the Commentary

"Love one another," John pointed out, was first true in Christ, and now it is true in the lives of those who are trusting Christ. Jesus Himself is the greatest example of this commandment.

Later on we will think about that great statement "God is love" (1 John 4:8), but it is anticipated here. When one looks at Jesus Christ, one sees love embodied and exemplified. In commanding us to love, Jesus does not ask us to do something that He has not already done Himself. The four gospel records are the account of a life lived in the spirit of love—and that life was lived under conditions far from ideal. Jesus says to us, in effect, "I lived by this great commandment, and I can enable you to follow My example."

Jesus illustrated love by the very life that He lived. He never showed hatred or malice. His righteous soul hated all sin and disobedience, but He never hated the people who committed such sins. Even in His righteous announcements of judgment, there was always an undercurrent of love.

It is encouraging to think of Jesus' love for the twelve disciples.

—*Be Real,* pages 56–57

6. Why is it important for John to note that the light is first seen in Jesus (1 John 2:8)? What are some specific examples of the love Jesus showed His disciples? What does it look like for Christians to express that kind of love toward others today?

From the Commentary

Perhaps the greatest thing about Jesus' love was the way it touched even the lives of His enemies. He looked with loving pity on the religious leaders who in their spiritual blindness accused Him of being in league with Satan (Matt. 12:24). When the mob came to arrest Him, He could have called on the armies of heaven for protection, but He yielded to His enemies. And then He died for them—for His enemies! "Greater love hath no man than this, that a man lay down his life for his friends" (John 15:13). But Jesus died not only for His friends, but also for

His foes! And as they crucified Him, He prayed for them: "Father, forgive them, for they know not what they do."

—*Be Real,* page 57

7. John stated that the truth is seen in Jesus and His followers because the "darkness is passing." What did he mean by this? How is loving enemies a way of bringing light to the world?

From the Commentary

It is easy to talk about Christian love, but much more difficult to practice it. For one thing, such love is not mere talk (1 John 2:9). For a Christian to say (or sing!) that he loves the brethren while he actually hates another believer is for him to lie. In other words (and this is a sobering truth), it is impossible to be in fellowship with the Father and out of fellowship with another Christian at the same time.

This is one reason why God established the local church, the fellowship of believers. "You can't be a Christian alone"; a person cannot live a complete and developing

Christian life unless he is in fellowship with God's people. The Christian life has two relationships: the vertical (Godward) and the horizontal (manward). And what God has joined together, man must not put asunder! And each of these two relationships is to be one of love one for the other.

Jesus dealt with this matter in the Sermon on the Mount (see Matt. 5:21–26). A gift on the altar was valueless as long as the worshipper had a dispute to settle with his brother. Note that Jesus did not say that the worshipper had something against his brother, but that the brother had something against the worshipper. But even when we have been offended, we should not wait for the one who has offended us to come to us; we should go to him. If we do not, Jesus warned us that we will end up in a prison of spiritual judgment where we will have to pay the last penny (Matt. 18:21–35). In other words, when we harbor an unforgiving, unloving spirit, we harm ourselves most.

—*Be Real,* pages 59–60

8. Review 1 John 2:9–11. How can hate blind people? What does this passage say about the hypocrisy of saying one thing and doing another?

From the Commentary

Christian love is not a shallow sentiment, a passing emotion that we perhaps experience in a church service. Christian love is a practical thing; it applies in the everyday affairs of life. Just consider the "one another" statements in the New Testament and you will see how practical it is to love one another. Here are just a few (there are over twenty such statements):

Wash one another's feet (John 13:14).

Prefer one another (Rom. 12:10).

Be of the same mind one to another (Rom. 12:16).

Do not judge one another (Rom. 14:13).

Receive one another (Rom. 15:7).

Admonish one another (Rom. 15:14).

Edify [build up] one another (1 Thess. 5:11).

Bear one another's burdens (Gal. 6:2).

Confess your faults to one another (James 5:16).

Use hospitality one to another (1 Peter 4:9).

In short, to love other Christians means to treat them the way God treats them—and the way God treats us. Christian love that does not show itself in action and in attitude is spurious (see 1 Cor. 13:4–7).

—*Be Real,* page 61

9. Review the passages listed above. How are these passages examples of living out the definition of love written in 1 Corinthians 13? Is it always easy to treat others in this way? Why or why not? What happens to a believer who doesn't love his or her brothers and sisters in Christ?

From the Commentary

> The Christian life—the life that is real—is a beautiful blending of "something old, something new." The Holy Spirit takes the "old things" and makes them "new things" in our experience. When you stop to think about it, the Holy Spirit never grows old! He is always young! And He is the only Person on earth today who was here centuries ago when Jesus lived, taught, died, and rose again. He is the only One who can take "old truth" and make it fresh and new in our daily experience at this present time.
>
> There are other exciting truths in the rest of John's letter, but if we fail to obey in this matter of love, the rest of the letter may well be "darkness" to us. Perhaps the best thing we can do, right now, is to search our hearts to see if we hold anything against a brother, or if someone has anything against us. The life that is real is an honest

life—and it is a life of doing, not merely saying. It is a life of active love in Christ. This means forgiveness, kindness, long-suffering. But it also means joy and peace and victory.

—*Be Real,* page 65

10. What are some of the "old things" that the Holy Spirit makes new when someone becomes a believer? What role does love for God and others play in these aspects of our lives? Is it possible to be a Christian and not love others? Explain.

Looking Inward

Take a moment to reflect on all that you've explored thus far in this study of 1 John 2:7–11. Review your notes and answers and think about how each of these things matters in your life today.

Tips for Small Groups: To get the most out of this section, form pairs or trios and have group members take turns answering these questions. Be honest and as open as you can in this discussion, but most of all, be encouraging and supportive of others. Be sensitive to those who are going through particularly difficult times and don't press for people to speak if they're uncomfortable doing so.

11. What is your definition of love? How has that definition changed over the years? What prompted that change? How has your faith informed your understanding of what love is?

12. Do you have friends you'd call "beloved"? What makes them beloved? In what ways are you a beloved friend to others?

13. How well do you practice what you preach when it comes to love? What are some ways your words and actions don't always line up? How can the message in 1 John help you learn how to live out your love in daily life?

Going Forward

14. Think of one or two things you have learned that you'd like to work on in the coming week. Remember that this is all about quality, not quantity. It's better to work on one specific area of life and do it well than to work on many and do poorly (or to be so overwhelmed that you simply don't try).

Do you need to work on matching your actions to your words? Take a difficult step of love? Be specific. Go back through 1 John 2:7–11 and put a star next to the phrase or verse that is most encouraging to you. Consider memorizing this verse.

Real-Life Application Ideas: Review the practical "one another" passages listed in the excerpt before question 9. Consider finding other such statements and add them to the list. Then consider practical, everyday ways to live out these statements. Look for ways to practice them at home, work, among friends and strangers, etc. Don't just make a commitment to "do better," but come up with specific plans for each. For example, "bear one another's burdens" might mean something like offering to take care of a neighbor's children for a weekend to give your neighbor a much-needed break.

Seeking Help

15. Write a prayer below (or simply pray one in silence), inviting God to work on your mind and heart in those areas you've noted above. Be honest about your desires and fears.

Notes for Small Groups:
- *Look for ways to put into practice the things you wrote in the Going Forward section. Talk with other group members about your ideas and commit to being accountable to one another.*
- *During the coming week, ask the Holy Spirit to continue to reveal truth to you from what you've read and studied.*
- *Before you start the next lesson, read 1 John 2:12–17. For more in-depth lesson preparation, read chapter 4, "The Love God Hates," in* Be Real.

The World
(1 JOHN 2:12–17)

Before you begin …
- *Pray for the Holy Spirit to reveal truth and wisdom as you go through this lesson.*
- *Read 1 John 2:12–17. This lesson references chapter 4 in* Be Real. *It will be helpful for you to have your Bible and a copy of the commentary available as you work through this lesson.*

Getting Started

From the Commentary

In more than one area of life, love and hate go hand in hand. A husband who loves his wife is certainly going to exercise a hatred for what would harm her. "Ye that love the LORD, hate evil" (Ps. 97:10). "Let love be without hypocrisy. Abhor what is evil; cling to what is good" (Rom. 12:9 NASB).

John's epistle has reminded us to exercise love (1 John

2:7–11)—the right kind of love. Now it warns us that there is a wrong kind of love, a love that God hates. This is love for what the Bible calls "the world."

—Be Real, page 69

1. John listed reasons for writing his letter in 1 John 2:12–14. What can you glean about the audience for the letter from these verses? How are these reasons applicable to us today?

More to Consider: How is worldliness defined today in Christian circles? What do non-Christians mean when they use the term worldly? *How does the familiar exhortation to be "in the world but not of it" relate to this passage?*

2. Choose one verse or phrase from 1 John 2:12–17 that stands out to you. This could be something you're intrigued by, something that makes you uncomfortable, something that puzzles you, something that resonates with you, or just something you want to examine further. Write that here.

Going Deeper

From the Commentary

> The New Testament word *world* has at least three different meanings. It sometimes means the physical world, the earth: "God that made the world [our planet] and all things therein" (Acts 17:24). It also means the human world, mankind: "For God so loved the world" (John 3:16). Sometimes these two ideas appear together: "He [Jesus] was in the world, and the world [earth] was made by him, and the world [mankind] knew him not" (1:10).
>
> But the warning "Love not the world!" is not about the world of nature or the world of men. Christians ought to appreciate the beauty and usefulness of the earth God has made, since He "giveth us richly all things to enjoy" (1 Tim. 6:17). And they certainly ought to love people— not only their friends, but even their enemies.
>
> —*Be Real,* pages 69–70

3. What did John mean by "the world" in 1 John 2:15–17? Why did he say, "Everything in the world … comes not from the Father but from the world"? What are some specific things in today's world that John would define as worldly?

From the Commentary

> Just as the Holy Spirit uses people to accomplish God's
> will on earth, so Satan uses people to fulfill his evil pur-
> poses. Unsaved people, whether they realize it or not, are
> energized by "the prince of the power of the air, the spirit
> that now worketh in the children of disobedience" (Eph.
> 2:1–2).
>
> —*Be Real,* page 70

4. How does Satan use unsaved people to fulfill his purposes? What are
some ways this may have played out in the days of the early church? How is
this in evidence today? How is the way Satan uses unsaved people different
from the way he tempts believers?

From the History Books

Some early Jewish religious groups around the time of Christ, including the
Essenes, removed themselves from the religious status quo and committed
their lives to asceticism, poverty, avoidance of worldly pleasures, and focus
on the study and understanding of Scriptures. In fact, it was the Essenes
who left behind what we now refer to as the Dead Sea Scrolls, ancient

papers that include our earliest recorded documentation of biblical and extrabiblical texts. Christian history has its share of groups who separate themselves from the world in pursuit of a purer biblical study, most notably monks from various orders around the world.

5. What prompts some people to try to separate themselves from the world? Is it truly possible to do this in modern society? Is it a healthy pursuit? Why or why not? What are the benefits of avoiding worldly things? What are the challenges? What wisdom can Christians who must live in the world glean from those who choose to live apart from it?

From the Commentary

"If any man love the world, the love of the Father is not in him" (1 John 2:15). Worldliness is not so much a matter of activity as of attitude. It is possible for a Christian to stay away from questionable amusements and doubtful places and still love the world, for worldliness is a matter of the heart. To the extent that a Christian loves the world system and the things in it, he does not love the Father.

Worldliness not only affects your response to the love of God; it also affects your response to the will of God. "The world passeth away … but he that doeth the will of God abideth forever" (1 John 2:17).

—*Be Real,* pages 71–72

6. Review 1 John 2:15–17. In what ways is worldliness an attitude? How is that reflected in actions? How does worldliness affect a Christian's response to God? How does it influence a believer's ability to see and follow God's will?

From the Commentary

John pointed out that the world system uses three devices to trap Christians: "the lust [desire] of the flesh, the lust of the eyes, and the pride of life" (1 John 2:16).

—*Be Real,* page 73

7. Read Genesis 3:6. How are the temptations John described in 1 John 2:16 similar to those that trapped Adam and Eve in the garden? How do the desires of the flesh, lust of the eyes, and pride of life trap believers? According to John, how can they avoid being trapped by these things?

From the Commentary

> This raises a practical and important question about the nature of a Christian and how he keeps from getting worldly.
>
> The answer is found in the unusual form of address used in 1 John 2:12–14. Note the titles used as John addressed his Christian readers: "little children ... fathers ... young men ... little children."
>
> What was he referring to?
>
> To begin with, "little children" (1 John 2:12) refers to all believers. Literally, this word means "born ones." All Christians have been born into God's family through faith in Jesus Christ, and their sins have been forgiven. The very fact that one is in God's family, sharing His nature, ought to discourage one from becoming friendly with the world. To be friendly with the world is treachery! "Friendship of the world is enmity with God ... whosoever therefore will be [wants to be] a friend of the world is the enemy of God" (James 4:4).
>
> —*Be Real,* page 77

8. What are some practical things a believer can do to keep from becoming worldly? How does spiritual growth help believers keep from falling into worldly ways? What are some of the things that help us grow up from "little children" into spiritually mature Christians?

More to Consider: Read 1 Corinthians 3:1–3. How do these verses speak to what John implied by his use of "little children" and "young men" in 1 John 2:12–14 (KJV)?

From the Commentary

"The world is passing away!" (see 1 John 2:17).

That statement would be challenged by many men today who are confident that the world—the system in which we live—is as permanent as anything can be. But the world is not permanent. The only sure thing about this world system is that it is not going to be here forever. One day the system will be gone, and the pleasant attractions within it will be gone.

—*Be Real,* pages 78–79

9. Why did John make the claim that the world is passing away? How is this in evidence today? Why might some people disagree with that statement? What are some ways the Bible reveals the impermanence of this world? What are the things that will outlast this world?

From the Commentary

> The New Testament has quite a bit to say about "the will of God." One of the "fringe benefits" of salvation is the privilege of knowing God's will (Acts 22:14). In fact, God wants us to be "filled with the knowledge of his will" (Col. 1:9). The will of God is not something that we consult occasionally like an encyclopedia. It is something that completely controls our lives. The issue for a dedicated Christian is not simply "Is it right or wrong?" or "Is it good or bad?" The key issue is "Is this the will of God for me?"
>
> God wants us to understand His will (Eph. 5:17), not just know what it is. "He made known his ways unto Moses, his acts unto the children of Israel" (Ps. 103:7). Israel knew what God was doing, but Moses knew why He was doing it! It is important that we understand God's will for our lives and see the purposes He is fulfilling.
>
> —*Be Real,* pages 80–81

10. What does John have to say about God's will in 1 John 2:17? What is "the will of God"? How are we to discover God's will? Read Ephesians 6:6 and Matthew 7:21. According to these verses, what are we to do once we understand God's will?

Looking Inward

Take a moment to reflect on all that you've explored thus far in this study of 1 John 2:12–17. Review your notes and answers and think about how each of these things matters in your life today.

Tips for Small Groups: To get the most out of this section, form pairs or trios and have group members take turns answering these questions. Be honest and as open as you can in this discussion, but most of all, be encouraging and supportive of others. Be sensitive to those who are going through particularly difficult times and don't press for people to speak if they're uncomfortable doing so.

11. What is your personal definition of *worldliness*? According to your definition, how worldly are you? Are you comfortable with the way you interact with the things of this world and how that intersects your faith? Explain.

12. Have you ever been sheltered from the world (or if you have children, have you sheltered them)? What was that experience like? In what ways is being sheltered a good thing? What are some of the disadvantages to being sheltered? How can faith grow in either situation?

13. What are some of the things you've done to grow up in your faith? In what ways do you see yourself still a child in matters of faith? How can you take steps to grow up in those areas?

Going Forward

14. Think of one or two things you have learned that you'd like to work on in the coming week. Remember that this is all about quality, not quantity. It's better to work on one specific area of life and do it well than to work on many and do poorly (or to be so overwhelmed that you simply don't try).

Do you need to learn how to have a less worldly attitude? Be specific. Go back through 1 John 2:12–17 and put a star next to the phrase or verse that is most encouraging to you. Consider memorizing this verse.

Real-Life Application Ideas: John's emphasis on avoiding worldliness was not incidental. Instead, it's foundational to his message of love. What are evidences in your life that you're avoiding worldliness? In what ways do you still have a worldly attitude? Take inventory of your attitudes and actions this coming week, paying special attention to those things that take your focus away from God. Then consider practical action to change your attitude so it's less worldly and more faith-minded. For example, if you find yourself drawn to mindless entertainment when you should be more focused on spending time with family, take steps to change that pattern.

Seeking Help

15. Write a prayer below (or simply pray one in silence), inviting God to work on your mind and heart in those areas you've noted above. Be honest about your desires and fears.

Notes for Small Groups:

- *Look for ways to put into practice the things you wrote in the Going Forward section. Talk with other group members about your ideas and commit to being accountable to one another.*

- *During the coming week, ask the Holy Spirit to continue to reveal truth to you from what you've read and studied.*

- *Before you start the next lesson, read 1 John 2:18–29. For more in-depth lesson preparation, read chapter 5, "Truth or Consequences," in* Be Real.

Truth
(1 JOHN 2:18–29)

Before you begin …
- *Pray for the Holy Spirit to reveal truth and wisdom as you go through this lesson.*
- *Read 1 John 2:18–29. This lesson references chapter 5 in* Be Real. *It will be helpful for you to have your Bible and a copy of the commentary available as you work through this lesson.*

Getting Started

From the Commentary

It takes more than "sincerity" to make something true. Faith in a lie will always cause serious consequences; faith in the truth is never misplaced. It does make a difference what a man believes! If a man wants to drive from Chicago to New York, no amount of sincerity will get him there if the highway is taking him to Los Angeles. A person who is real builds his life on truth, not superstition or lies. It is impossible to live a real life by believing lies.

God has warned the church family ("little children") about the conflict between light and darkness (1 John 1:1—2:6) and between love and hatred (2:7–17). Now He warns them about a third conflict: the conflict between truth and error. It is not enough for a believer to walk in the light and to walk in love; he must also walk in truth. The issue is truth—or consequences!

—*Be Real,* pages 87–88

1. How do believers determine the difference between truth and lies? In practical terms, how does a Christian come to understand the truth available in the Bible? What are the foundational truths that John wrote about in 1 John 2:18–29?

2. Choose one verse or phrase from 1 John 2:18–29 that stands out to you. This could be something you're intrigued by, something that makes you uncomfortable, something that puzzles you, something that resonates with you, or just something you want to examine further. Write that here.

Going Deeper

From the Commentary

Before John explained the tragic consequences of turning from the truth, he emphasized the seriousness of the matter. He did so by using two special terms: "the last time" and "antichrist." Both terms make it clear that Christians are living in an hour of crisis and must guard against the errors of the enemy.

"The last time" (or "the last hour") is a term that reminds us that a new age has dawned on the world. "The darkness is past, and the true light now shineth" (1 John 2:8)....

The second term, "antichrist," is used in the Bible only by John (1 John 2:18, 22; 4:3; 2 John 7). It describes three things: (1) a spirit in the world that opposes or denies Christ; (2) the false teachers who embody this spirit; and (3) a person who will head up the final world rebellion against Christ.

—*Be Real,* pages 88–89

3. John's message about the truth uses dramatic language. Why do you think he referred to those who deny that Jesus is God's Son as "antichrists"? Why such a pointed term? What might this suggest about the challenges of the early church? How is it equally applicable as a warning for Christians today?

More to Consider: The prefix anti- *has a dual meaning. In Greek, it can mean both "against" Christ and "instead of" Christ. How can the term* antichrist *use both definitions?*

From the Commentary

John's epistle gives three outstanding marks of the false teacher who is controlled by the "spirit of antichrist."

The first is that the false teacher departs from the fellowship (1 John 2:18–19). "They went out from us, but they were not really of us; for if they had been of us, they would have remained with us" (v. 19 NASB).

The word *us* refers, of course, to the fellowship of believers, the church. Not everyone who is part of an assembly of believers is necessarily a member of the family of God!

The New Testament presents the church in a twofold way: as one worldwide family and as local units or assemblies of believers. There is a "universal" as well as "local" aspect of the church. The whole worldwide company of believers is compared with a body (1 Cor. 12) and with a building (Eph. 2:19–22). When a sinner trusts Christ as Savior, he receives eternal life and immediately becomes a member of God's family and a part of Christ's spiritual body. He should then identify himself with a local group of Christians (a church) and start serving Christ (Acts 2:41–42). But the point here is that a person can belong to a local church and not be part of the true spiritual body of Christ.

—Be Real, page 90

4. Why would John make a point to note that those who "went out from us" never really "belonged to us" (1 John 2:19)? What does it mean for someone to "belong" to a church in this sense? What are valid reasons for departing from a congregation? What are invalid reasons?

From Today's World

The early church was primarily a "home church" that met wherever people could find room. It wasn't until later that congregations began to designate places of worship. Today, the word *church* is probably used more in reference to a building than the people. But while megachurches continue to grow and draw crowds every week, there has also been a resurgence of interest in the "home church" concept. Whether the reason is dissatisfaction with traditional church or simply a desire to go small, small group meetings held in homes or coffee shops are fast becoming the face of the new church for many believers.

5. What is appealing about the "home church" concept? What unique needs can a small group provide that a larger congregation can't? What are a small church's unique ministry opportunities? What are some of the disadvantages or challenges facing home churches or smaller congregations? How can John's message about "belonging" apply to all kinds of churches?

From the Commentary

> There are many unfortunate divisions among the people of God today, but all true Christians have things in common, regardless of church affiliation. They believe that the Bible is the Word of God and that Jesus is the Son of God. They confess that men are sinners and that the only way one can be saved is through faith in Christ. They believe that Christ died as man's substitute on the cross, and that He arose again from the dead. They believe that the Holy Spirit indwells true believers. Finally, they believe that one day in the future Jesus will come again. Christians may differ on other matters—church government, for example, or modes of baptism—but they agree on the basic doctrines of the faith.

If you will investigate the history of the false cults and anti-Christian religious systems in today's world, you will find that in most cases their founders started out in a local church! They were "with us" but not "of us," so they went out "from us" and started their own groups.

Any group, no matter how "religious," that for doctrinal reasons separates itself from a local church that holds to the Word of God, must immediately be suspect. Often these groups follow human leaders and the books men have written, rather than Jesus Christ and God's Word.

—*Be Real,* page 91

6. Why are churches so easily divided? What are some of the main reasons for division and conflict? Review 2 Timothy 3—4 and 2 Peter 2. What do these passages teach about the dangers of departing from the fellowship? How can the local church deal with contentious issues in a way that brings people together instead of pushing them apart? Are there times when separation is the best answer? Explain.

From the Commentary

> The key questions for a Christian are Who is Jesus Christ? Is Christ merely "an example," "a good Man," or "a wonderful teacher"; or is He God come in the flesh?
>
> John's readers knew the truth about Christ, or else they would not have been saved. You all know the truth, because you have the Spirit of God, an unction, and the Spirit teaches you all things (see 1 John 2:20, 27). "Now if any man have not the Spirit of Christ, he is none of his" (Rom. 8:9).
>
> False Christians in John's day used two special words to describe their experience: *knowledge* and *unction*. They claimed to have a special unction (anointing) from God that gave them a unique knowledge. They were "illuminated" and therefore living on a much higher level than anybody else. But John pointed out that all true Christians know God and have received the Spirit of God! And because they have believed the truth, they recognize a lie when they meet it.
>
> —*Be Real,* page 92

7. Read 1 John 4:2. How does the truth of this verse set Christians apart from others? Why is the sonship of Christ critical to Christianity? What warnings did John give for those who deny Jesus is God's Son?

From the Commentary

> It is important that you stay with the truth of God's Word.
> The Word (or message) Christians have "heard from the
> beginning" is all you need to keep you true to the faith.
> The Christian life continues just as it began: through
> faith in the Bible's message. A religious leader who comes
> along with "something new," something that contradicts
> what Christians have "heard from the beginning," is not
> to be trusted. "Try the spirits, whether they are of God"
> (1 John 4:1). Let the Word abide in you (2:24), and abide
> in Christ (2:28); otherwise you will be led astray by the
> spirit of antichrist. No matter what false teachers may
> promise, you have the sure promise of eternal life (v. 25).
> You need nothing more!
>
> —*Be Real,* pages 93–94

8. Review 1 John 2:24–27. What are the things that we "have heard from
the beginning"? What role do tradition and history play in our faith? Why
is it important to test new theologies or beliefs against the long-held ones?
How do believers discern potentially heretical or misleading beliefs?

More to Consider: It is interesting to observe that anti-Christian groups rarely try to lead lost sinners to their false faiths. Instead, they spend much of their time trying to convert professing Christians (and church members, at that) to their own doctrines. Why do you think this is true? In what ways are practicing Christians a more logical target for anti-Christian groups than lost sinners? What are practical ways to guard against these anti-Christian groups' tactics?

From the Commentary

Satan is not an originator; he is a counterfeiter. He imitates the work of God. For example, Satan has counterfeit "ministers" (2 Cor. 11:13–15) who preach a counterfeit gospel (Gal. 1:6–12) that produces counterfeit Christians (John 8:43–44) who depend on a counterfeit righteousness (Rom. 10:1–10). In the parable of the tares (Matt. 13:24–30, 36–43), Jesus and Satan are pictured as sowers. Jesus sows the true seed, the children of God, but Satan sows "the children of the wicked one." The two kinds of plants, while growing, look so much alike that the servants could not tell the difference until the fruit appeared! Satan's chief stratagem during this age is to plant the counterfeit wherever Christ plants the true. And it is important that you be able to detect the counterfeit and separate the teachings of Christ from the false teachings of antichrist.

—*Be Real*, pages 94–95

9. Read John 14:17 and 1 John 4:2–3, 6. How can Christians detect counterfeit teachings? What role does the Holy Spirit play in our ability to identify the difference between truth and lies? What role does the Bible play? Other believers?

From the Commentary

It is possible to be a child in a family and yet be out of fellowship with one's father and with other members of the family. When our heavenly Father discovers that we are out of fellowship with Him, He deals with us to bring us back into the place of abiding. This process is called "chastening"—child training (Heb. 12:5–11).

A believer must allow the Spirit of God to teach him from the Bible. One of the major functions of a local church is the teaching of God's Word (2 Tim. 2:2; 4:1–5). The Spirit gives the gift of teaching to certain individuals in the fellowship (Rom. 12:6–7) and they teach others, but what they teach must be tested (1 John 4:1–3)....

When Apollos preached in the synagogue at Ephesus, his message was correct as far as it went, but it was not complete. Priscilla and Aquila, two mature believers in the congregation, took him aside privately and instructed him in the full message of Christ (Acts 18:24–28). A Christian who spends time daily in the Bible and in prayer will walk in the Spirit and have the discernment he needs.

—Be Real, page 97

10. What's the difference between deliberate deception and spiritual ignorance? What's the church's responsibility in dealing with each of these?

Looking Inward

Take a moment to reflect on all that you've explored thus far in this study of 1 John 2:18–29. Review your notes and answers and think about how each of these things matters in your life today.

Tips for Small Groups: To get the most out of this section, form pairs or trios and have group members take turns answering these questions. Be honest and as open as you can in this discussion, but most of all, be encouraging and supportive of others. Be sensitive to those who are going through particularly difficult times and don't press for people to speak if they're uncomfortable doing so.

11. How certain are you that you are following the truth and not being led astray by false teaching? What are some of the clues that tell you when a particular belief isn't aligned with truth? What do you do when you encounter a questionable belief?

12. Have you ever been an "antichrist" in the past? If so, in what ways? What are some of the attitudes or actions you've practiced that go against God's truth? How did you move away from those false teachings?

13. Describe your current church affiliation. In what ways are you practicing what John teaches about belonging? What are some of the things you most

love about your current church situation? What are some things you wish you could change? How might you go about doing that in a loving way?

Going Forward

14. Think of one or two things you have learned that you'd like to work on in the coming week. Remember that this is all about quality, not quantity. It's better to work on one specific area of life and do it well than to work on many and do poorly (or to be so overwhelmed that you simply don't try).

Do you want to sort through some possibly false teaching? Do you want to address division within the church? Be specific. Go back through 1 John 2:18–29 and put a star next to the phrase or verse that is most encouraging to you. Consider memorizing this verse.

Real-Life Application Ideas: Take stock of your current church situation. In what ways are you making the most of your church experience? What are some ways you could invest yourself in the lives of others in your congregation? Look for practical ideas—like leading a small group or volunteering to help set up the auditorium or hosting coffee chats with people outside of your normal social circles.

Seeking Help

15. Write a prayer below (or simply pray one in silence), inviting God to work on your mind and heart in those areas you've noted above. Be honest about your desires and fears.

Notes for Small Groups:

- *Look for ways to put into practice the things you wrote in the Going Forward section. Talk with other group members about your ideas and commit to being accountable to one another.*

- *During the coming week, ask the Holy Spirit to continue to reveal truth to you from what you've read and studied.*

- *Before you start the next lesson, read 1 John 3:1–10. For more in-depth lesson preparation, read chapter 6, "The Pretenders," in* Be Real.

The Pretenders
(I JOHN 3:1–10)

Before you begin …
- *Pray for the Holy Spirit to reveal truth and wisdom as you go through this lesson.*
- *Read 1 John 3:1–10. This lesson references chapter 6 in* Be Real. *It will be helpful for you to have your Bible and a copy of the commentary available as you work through this lesson.*

Getting Started

From the Commentary

> The United States Treasury Department has a special group of men whose job it is to track down counterfeiters. Naturally, these men need to know a counterfeit bill when they see it.
>
> How do they learn to identify fake bills?
>
> Oddly enough, they are not trained by spending hours examining counterfeit money. Rather, they study the

real thing. They become so familiar with authentic bills that they can spot a counterfeit by looking at it or, often, simply by feeling it.

This is the approach in 1 John 3, which warns us that in today's world there are counterfeit Christians—"children of the devil" (1 John 3:10). But instead of listing the evil characteristics of Satan's children, the Scripture gives us a clear description of God's children. The contrast between the two is obvious.

—*Be Real*, page 105

1. Why do you think John chose to focus on the positive in this chapter in his description of God's children? How is this approach in direct contrast to much of the rest of Scripture, where writers went into great detail about the characteristics of a sinful life? What are some of the direct inferences readers can make about Satan's children from the message in 1 John 3?

More to Consider: The key verse of this chapter is 1 John 3:10: A true child of God practices righteousness and loves other Christians despite differences. What does this mean in practical terms? How can you practice righteousness when you disagree with other Christians?

2. Choose one verse or phrase from 1 John 3:1–10 that stands out to you. This could be something you're intrigued by, something that makes you uncomfortable, something that puzzles you, something that resonates with you, or just something you want to examine further. Write that here.

Going Deeper

From the Commentary

> Practicing righteousness and loving the brethren, of course, are not new themes. These two important subjects are treated in the first two chapters of this epistle, but in 1 John 3 the approach is different. In the first two chapters the emphasis was on fellowship: A Christian who is in fellowship with God will practice righteousness and will love the brethren. But in 1 John 3—5, the emphasis is on sonship: Because a Christian is "born of God," he will practice righteousness and will love the brethren.
>
> —*Be Real,* pages 105–6

3. Read 1 John 2:29; 3:9; 4:7; 5:1, 4, 18. What are the qualities of one who is "born of God"? Why does being born of God lead to these qualities? Does this happen automatically, or does it require effort on our parts? Describe the process as you understand it.

From the Commentary

Every great personality mentioned in the Bible sinned at one time or another. Abraham lied about his wife (Gen. 12:10–20). Moses lost his temper and disobeyed God (Num. 20:7–13). Peter denied the Lord three times (Matt. 26:69–75). But sin was not the settled practice of these men. It was an incident in their lives, totally contrary to their normal habits. And when they sinned, they confessed it and asked God to forgive them.

An unsaved person (even if he professes to be a Christian but is a counterfeit) lives a life of habitual sin. Sin—especially the sin of unbelief—is the normal thing in his life (Eph. 2:1–3). He has no divine resources to draw on. His profession of faith, if any, is not real. This is the distinction in view in 1 John 3:1–10—a true believer does not live in habitual sin. He may commit sin—an occasional wrong act—but he will not practice sin—make a settled habit of it.

The difference is that a true Christian knows God. A counterfeit Christian may talk about God and get involved in "religious activities," but he does not really know God. The person who has been "born of God" through faith in Christ knows God the Father, God the Son, and God the Holy Spirit. And because he knows them, he lives a life of obedience: He does not practice sin.

—*Be Real,* pages 106–7

4. Why is unbelief considered a sin? What are some examples in modern society that illustrate the truth that people can know about God and yet not be true Christians? What does it mean to truly "know" God? According to John, how is that in evidence in a believer's life?

From the Commentary

God's love for us is unique. First John 3:1 may be translated, "Behold, what peculiar, out-of-this-world kind of love the Father has bestowed on us." While we were His enemies, God loved us and sent His Son to die for us!

The whole wonderful plan of salvation begins with the love of God.

Many translators add a phrase to 1 John 3:1: "That we should be called the sons of God, and we are." "Sons of God" is not simply a high-sounding name that we bear; it is a reality! We are God's children! We do not expect the world to understand this thrilling relationship, because it does not even understand God. Only a person who knows God through Christ can fully appreciate what it means to be called a child of God.

—*Be Real,* page 107

5. What makes God's love for us so unique? If 1 John 3:1 tells us what we are, what does 1 John 3:2 tell us about who we'll be someday? What does John mean when he says that "we shall be like [Christ], for we shall see him as he is"?

From the Commentary

> In 1 John 3:3, John told us what we should be. In view of
> the return of Jesus Christ, we should keep our lives clean.
>
> All this is to remind us of the Father's love. Because the
> Father loved us and sent His Son to die for us, we are
> children of God. Because God loves us, He wants us to
> live with Him one day. Salvation, from start to finish,
> is an expression of the love of God. We are saved by the
> grace of God (Eph. 2:8–9; Titus 2:11–15), but the provi-
> sion for our salvation was originated in the love of God.
> And since we have experienced the love of the Father, we
> have no desire to live in sin.
>
> —*Be Real,* pages 107–8

6. What is the purity John referred to in 1 John 3:3? How can we become
pure? Respond to this statement: "An unbeliever who sins is a creature
sinning against his Creator. A Christian who sins is a child sinning against
his Father." What difference does that make in practice?

From the Commentary

> In 1 John 3:4–8, John turned from the future appearing
> of Jesus (v. 2) to His past appearing (v. 5, where the word
> *manifest* means "appear"). John gave two reasons why
> Jesus came and died: (1) to take away our sins (vv. 4–6),
> and (2) to destroy the works of the Devil (vv. 7–8). For a
> child of God to sin indicates that he does not understand
> or appreciate what Jesus did for him on the cross.
>
> —*Be Real*, pages 108–9

7. Review 1 John 3:4–8. What are believers supposed to take away from
this passage? What does it mean to no longer continue in sin? How is that
different from being sinless?

From the Commentary

> "Whosoever abideth in him" does not practice sin (1 John
> 3:6). "Abide" was one of John's favorite words. To abide
> in Christ means to be in fellowship with Him, to allow
> nothing to come between ourselves and Christ. Sonship

(being born of God) brings about our union with Christ, but fellowship makes possible our communion with Christ. It is this communion (abiding) with Christ that keeps us from deliberately disobeying His Word.

A person who deliberately and habitually sins is proving that he does not know Christ and therefore cannot be abiding in Him.

—*Be Real,* page 110

8. Does habitual sin prove that someone doesn't know Christ? Can someone know Jesus and still wrestle with habitual sin? Explain.

More to Consider: Read Isaiah 14:9–17 and Ezekiel 28:12–14. What do these passages tell us about the possible origin of Satan? How does sin factor into this explanation?

From the Commentary

"Whosoever is born of God does not practice sin!"

Why? Because he has a new nature within him, and that new nature cannot sin. John called this new nature God's "seed."

When a person receives Christ as his Savior, tremendous spiritual changes take place in him. He is given a new standing before God, being accepted as righteous in God's sight. This new standing is called "justification." It never changes and is never lost.

The new Christian is also given a new position: He is set apart for God's own purposes to live for His glory. This new position is called "sanctification," and it has a way of changing from day to day. On some days we are much closer to Christ and obey Him much more readily.

But perhaps the most dramatic change in a new believer is what we call "regeneration." He is "born again" into the family of God. (*Re-* means "again," and *generation* means "birth.")

Justification means a new standing before God, sanctification means being set apart to God, and regeneration means a new nature—God's nature (see 2 Peter 1:4).

The only way to enter God's family is by trusting Christ and experiencing this new birth. "Whosoever believeth that Jesus is the Christ is born of God" (1 John 5:1).

Physical life produces only physical life; spiritual life produces spiritual life.

—*Be Real,* pages 112–13

9. Review 1 John 3:9–10. How does a "born of God" Christian's new nature reveal itself in daily living? How do we do things differently if we truly know ourselves to be set apart?

From the Commentary

Yielding to sin is the distinguishing mark of "the children of the devil" (1 John 3:10). They profess, or claim, one thing, but they practice another. Satan is a liar and the father of lies (John 8:44), and his children are like their father. "He that saith, 'I know [God],' and keepeth not his commandments, is a liar, and the truth is not in him" (1 John 2:4). The children of the Devil try to deceive God's children into thinking that a person can be a Christian and still practice sin. "Little children, let no man deceive you; he that doeth righteousness is righteous, even as he [God] is righteous" (3:7).

False teachers in John's day taught that a Christian did not have to worry about sin, because only the body sinned and what the body did in no way affected the spirit. Some of them went so far as to teach that sin is natural to the body, because the body is sinful.

The New Testament exposes the foolishness of such excuses for sin.

To begin with, "the old nature" is not the body. The body itself is neutral: It can be used either by the old sinful nature or by the new divine nature. "Therefore do not let sin reign in your mortal body so that you obey its lusts, and do not go on presenting the members of your body to sin as instruments of unrighteousness; but present yourselves to God as those [who are] alive from the dead, and your members as instruments of righteousness to God" (Rom. 6:12–13 NASB).

—Be Real, pages 116–17

10. How does a child of God go about overcoming the desires of the old nature? What does it mean to daily yield your body to Christ? (See Rom. 12:1.) How can believers feed their new nature?

Looking Inward

Take a moment to reflect on all that you've explored thus far in this study of 1 John 3:1–10. Review your notes and answers and think about how each of these things matters in your life today.

Tips for Small Groups: To get the most out of this section, form pairs or trios and have group members take turns answering these questions. Be honest and as open as you can in this discussion, but most of all, be encouraging and supportive of others. Be sensitive to those who are going through particularly difficult times and don't press for people to speak if they're uncomfortable doing so.

11. What are some ways you are like the "children of God" John described in 1 John 3? What does it mean to you to be considered a child of God? How does being God's child affect the way you live? How do you want it to affect you?

12. What's the first thing that comes to mind when you hear the word *purity*? What is John's definition of purity? What are some ways you pursue purity? What are the obstacles in your way? What are steps you can take to overcome those obstacles?

13. Do you struggle with habits of sin? How are you dealing with those struggles? How can focusing more on your constant connection to Christ ("abiding") help you deal with the temptation to continue in sin?

Going Forward

14. Think of one or two things you have learned that you'd like to work on in the coming week. Remember that this is all about quality, not quantity. It's better to work on one specific area of life and do it well than to work on many and do poorly (or to be so overwhelmed that you simply don't try).

Do you need to draw on Christ to break a sinful habit? Do you want to know how to better embrace your "new nature" in Christ? Be specific. Go back through 1 John 3:1–10 and put a star next to the phrase or verse that is most encouraging to you. Consider memorizing this verse.

Real-Life Application Ideas: First John 3:1 tells of God's great love for us. Take time this week to think about what it means to be so loved by God. Then celebrate that love in practical ways that honor God. For example, you could pass along God's love in a palpable way to someone who's hurting by spending time with him or her, participate in private or public worship, or tell a nonbelieving friend about what it feels like to be loved by God. Express your thanks toward God with your actions.

Seeking Help

15. Write a prayer below (or simply pray one in silence), inviting God to work on your mind and heart in those areas you've noted above. Be honest about your desires and fears.

Notes for Small Groups:

- *Look for ways to put into practice the things you wrote in the Going Forward section. Talk with other group members about your ideas and commit to being accountable to one another.*

- *During the coming week, ask the Holy Spirit to continue to reveal truth to you from what you've read and studied.*

- *Before you start the next lesson, read 1 John 3:11–24. For more in-depth lesson preparation, read chapter 7, "Love or Death," in* Be Real.

A Matter of Life and Death
(1 JOHN 3:11–24)

Before you begin …
- *Pray for the Holy Spirit to reveal truth and wisdom as you go through this lesson.*
- *Read 1 John 3:11–24. This lesson references chapter 7 in* Be Real. *It will be helpful for you to have your Bible and a copy of the commentary available as you work through this lesson.*

Getting Started

From the Commentary

John's letter has been compared to a spiral staircase because he kept returning to the same three topics: love, obedience, and truth. Though these themes recur, it is not true that they are merely repetitious. Each time we return to a topic, we look at it from a different point of view and are taken more deeply into it.

We have already learned about our love for other

believers—"the brethren" (1 John 2:7–11)—but the emphasis in 1 John 2 is on fellowship. A believer who is "walking in the light" will evidence that fact by loving the brethren. In our present section, the emphasis is on his relationship with other believers.

Christians love one another because they have all been born of God, which makes them all brothers and sisters in Christ.

Obedience and love are both evidences of sonship and brotherhood. We have been reminded that a true child of God practices righteousness (1 John 3:1–10), and now we shall look into the matter of love for the brethren (vv. 11–24). This truth is first stated in the negative: "Whosoever doeth not righteousness is not of God, neither he that loveth not his brother" (v. 10).

A striking difference should be noted between the earlier and the present treatment of love for the brethren. In the section on fellowship (1 John 2:7–11), we are told that loving the brethren is a matter of light and darkness. If we do not love one another, we cannot walk in the light, no matter how loud our profession. But in this section (3:11–24), the epistle probes much deeper.

—*Be Real,* pages 121–22

1. In what ways is 1 John 3:11–24 about brotherhood? Why is loving the brethren a matter of life and death?

Lesson 6: A Matter of Life and Death / 93

phrase from 1 John 3:11–24 that stands out to you.
g you're intrigued by, something that makes you
ng that puzzles you, something that resonates with
ou want to examine further. Write that here.

Going Deeper

From the Commentary

> When it comes to this matter of love, there are four possible
> "levels of relationship," so to speak, on which a person may
> live: murder (1 John 3:11–12), hatred (vv. 13–15), indiffer-
> ence (vv. 16–17), and Christian compassion (vv. 18–24).
>
> The first two are not Christian at all, the third is less
> than Christian, and only the last is compatible with true
> Christian love.
>
> *—Be Real,* page 122

3. How did John address the various levels of relationship in 1 John
3:11–24? What did he mean when he wrote, "Anyone who does not love
remains in death" (v. 14)?

From the Commentary

Murder, of course, is the lowest level on which one may live in relationship to someone else. It is the level on which Satan himself exists. The Devil was a murderer from the beginning of his fallen career (John 8:44), but Christians have heard, from the beginning of their experience, that they are to "love one another." John emphasized origins: "Go back to the beginning." If our spiritual experience originates with the Father, we must love one another. But if it originates with Satan, we will hate one another. "Let that therefore abide in you which ye have heard from the beginning" (1 John 2:24).

Cain is an example of a life of hatred; we find the record in Genesis 4:1–16. It is important to note that Cain and Abel, being brothers, had the same parents, and they both brought sacrifices to God. Cain is not presented as an atheist; he is presented as a worshipper. And this is the point: Children of the Devil masquerade as true believers. They attend religious gatherings, as Cain did. They may even bring offerings. But these actions in themselves are not valid proof that a man is born of God. The real test is his love for the brethren—and here Cain failed.

Every man has a "spiritual lineage" as well as a physical, and Cain's "spiritual father" was the Devil. This does not mean, of course, that Satan literally fathered Cain. It means, rather, that Cain's attitudes and actions originated with Satan. Cain was a murderer and a liar like Satan (John 8:44). He murdered his brother, and then he lied about it. "And the LORD said unto Cain, Where is Abel thy brother? And he said, I know not" (Gen. 4:9).

—*Be Real,* pages 122–23

4. John said believers are not to be like Cain because he "belonged to the evil one" (1 John 3:12). What does it mean to "belong to the evil one"? What are the signs (apart from the action of murder as in Cain's case) that someone belongs to Satan? How do we determine which actions are evil?

From Today's World

One of the popular catchwords in culture today is *tolerance.* Whether it's being wielded in social circles or political circles, the word has gained almost universal acclaim. And why not? Tolerance at its heart is a good thing, promising acceptance of people no matter what their beliefs or circumstances, offering an answer to such detestable actions as hate crimes and bullying. Jesus certainly practiced love of all people when He walked the earth. But tolerance and unconditional love are two different things.

5. What is the difference between tolerance and the sort of love Jesus practiced and taught us about? How does unconditional love respond to

such things as hate crimes and bullying? Is tolerance a bad thing? Explain. What would John say to those who preach tolerance today?

From the Commentary

> Cain's attitude represents the attitude of the present world system (1 John 3:13). The world hates Christ (John 15:18–25) for the same reason Cain hated Abel: Christ shows up the world's sin and reveals its true nature. When the world, like Cain, comes face-to-face with reality and truth, it can make only one of two decisions: Repent and change, or destroy the one who is exposing it.
>
> —*Be Real,* page 124

6. What is the world's true nature? What evidence do we have that the world hates Jesus today? Why did John say, "Do not be surprised … if the world hates you" (1 John 3:13)?

From the Commentary

At this point, you are probably thinking, "But I have never murdered anyone!" And to this statement, God replies, "Yes, but remember that to a Christian hatred is the same as murder" (1 John 3:15; cf. Matt. 5:22). The only difference between Level 1 and Level 2 is the outward act of taking life. The inward intent is the same.

A visitor at the zoo was chatting with the keeper of the lion house.

"I have a cat at home," said the visitor, "and your lions act just like my cat. Look at them sleeping so peacefully! It seems a shame that you have to put those beautiful creatures behind bars."

"My friend," the keeper laughed, "these may look like your cat, but their disposition is radically different. There's murder in their hearts. You'd better be glad the bars are there."

The only reason some people have never actually murdered anyone is because of the "bars" that have been put up: the fear of arrest and shame, the penalties of the law, and the possibility of death. But we are going to be judged by "the law of liberty" (James 2:12). The question is not so much "What did you do?" but "What did you want to do? What would you have done if you had been at liberty to do as you pleased?" This is why Jesus equated hatred with murder (Matt. 5:21–26) and lust with adultery (vv. 27–30).

This does not mean, of course, that hatred in the heart does the same amount of damage, or involves the same degree of guilt, as actual murder. Your neighbor would rather you hate him than kill him! But in God's sight, hatred is the moral equivalent of murder, and if left unbridled it leads to murder. A Christian has passed from death to life (John 5:24), and the proof of this is that he loves the brethren. When he belonged to the world system, he hated God's people, but now that he belongs to God, he loves them.

—*Be Real,* pages 124–25

7. Respond to this statement: "Hatred is the moral equivalent of murder." Do you agree? Why or why not? Why did John speak so strongly about hatred? What is the difference between hatred and anger? (See Matt. 5:22–24.) How are believers supposed to deal with their anger toward one another? (See Eph. 4:20–27.)

From the Commentary

> Hatred does the hater far more damage than it does anyone else (Matt. 5:21–26). Jesus said that anger put a man in danger of facing the local court. Calling a brother an "empty-headed fool" put him in danger of the Sanhedrin, the highest Jewish council. But calling him a "cursed fool" put him in danger of eternal judgment in hell. Hatred that is not confessed and forsaken actually puts a man into a spiritual and emotional prison (v. 25)!
>
> —*Be Real,* page 126

8. In what ways is love the antidote for hatred? How does Jesus turn a hateful heart to a loving heart? What does Jesus' action on the cross teach us about the manner in which we should love others (1 John 3:16)? If we feel hatred toward someone, how can we address the roots that are feeding that hatred?

From the Commentary

But the test of Christian love is not simply failure to do evil to others. Love also involves doing them good. Christian love is both positive and negative. "Cease to do evil; learn to do well" (Isa. 1:16–17).

Cain is our example of false love; Christ is the example of true Christian love. Jesus gave His life for us that we may experience truth. Every Christian knows John 3:16, but how many of us pay much attention to 1 John 3:16? It is wonderful to experience the blessing of John 3:16, but it is even more wonderful to share that experience by obeying 1 John 3:16: Christ "laid down life for us: and we ought to lay down our lives for the brethren."

Christian love involves sacrifice and service. Christ did not simply talk about His love; He died to prove it (Rom. 5:6–10). Jesus was not killed as a martyr; He willingly laid down His life (John 10:11–18; 15:13). "Self-preservation" is the first law of physical life, but "self-sacrifice" is the first law of spiritual life.

But God does not ask us to lay down our lives. He simply asks us to help a brother in need. John wisely turned from "the brethren" in 1 John 3:16 to the singular, "his brother," in 1 John 3:17.

It is easy for us to talk about "loving the brethren" and to neglect to help a single other believer. Christian love is personal and active....

If I am going to help my brother, I must meet three conditions. First, I must have the means necessary to meet his need. Second, I must know that the need exists. Third, I must be loving enough to want to share.

—*Be Real,* pages 126–28

9. What's wrong with indifference (1 John 3:16–17)? Why is it such a dangerous attitude to hold? What are the factors in our lives that foster indifference toward others? How is Christian love personal and active? What are examples of that kind of love?

More to Consider: In these days of multiplied social agencies helping people, it is easy for Christians to forget their obligations. Read Galatians 6:10. What does this verse tell us about how our love ought to be expressed in action?

From the Commentary

True Christian love means loving in deed and in truth. The opposite of "in deed" is "in word," and the opposite of "in truth" is "in tongue." Here is an example of love "in word": "If a brother or sister is without clothing and in need of daily food, and one of you says to them, 'Go in peace, be warmed and be filled,' and yet you do not give them what is necessary for their body, what use is that?" (James 2:15–16 NASB).

To love "in word" means simply to talk about a need, but to love "in deed" means to do something about meeting it. You may think, because you have discussed a need, or even prayed about it, that you have done your duty, but love involves more than words—it calls for sacrificial deeds.

To love "in tongue" is the opposite of to love "in truth." It means to love insincerely. To love "in truth" means to love a person genuinely from the heart and not just from the tongue. People are attracted by genuine love, but repelled by the artificial variety. One reason why sinners were attracted to Jesus (Luke 15:1–2) was because they were sure He loved them sincerely.

—*Be Real,* page 129

10. What's the motivation for our love of others? What is the cost of loving with our actions and not just our words? What are the blessings John described that will come to believers who practice Christian love? (See 1 John 3:19–22.)

Looking Inward

Take a moment to reflect on all that you've explored thus far in this study of 1 John 3:11–24. Review your notes and answers and think about how each of these things matters in your life today.

Tips for Small Groups: To get the most out of this section, form pairs or trios and have group members take turns answering these questions. Be honest and as open as you can in this discussion, but most of all, be encouraging and supportive of others. Be sensitive to those who are going through particularly difficult times and don't press for people to speak if they're uncomfortable doing so.

11. Have you ever felt angry enough with someone that you wished he or she were dead? What prompted that anger? How did you resolve that situation? What do you think is a constructive way to deal with your anger?

12. In what ways do you practice indifference? Why are you indifferent in those specific situations or toward those specific people? What would it look like to turn your indifference into love? What would that require from you?

13. Do you love more with words or actions? Explain. How do you express your love for others through your actions? What are some ways you can be more loving with your actions?

Going Forward

14. Think of one or two things you have learned that you'd like to work on in the coming week. Remember that this is all about quality, not quantity. It's better to work on one specific area of life and do it well than to work on many and do poorly (or to be so overwhelmed that you simply don't try).

Do you want to love more through your actions? Do you want to let God show you why you are so often indifferent? Be specific. Go back through 1 John 3:11–24 and put a star next to the phrase or verse that is most encouraging to you. Consider memorizing this verse.

Real-Life Application Ideas: One of John's points about love is that we're to help meet each other's needs, whatever those needs might be. Take a look at your material possessions. Are there some things you can give to others that will show love for them? Perhaps you have clothing you can donate to those in need. Maybe a neighbor could use your carpentry or baking skills. Look for practical ways to show your love through action and enact those this week.

Seeking Help

15. Write a prayer below (or simply pray one in silence), inviting God to work on your mind and heart in those areas you've noted above. Be honest about your desires and fears.

Notes for Small Groups:

- *Look for ways to put into practice the things you wrote in the Going Forward section. Talk with other group members about your ideas and commit to being accountable to one another.*

- *During the coming week, ask the Holy Spirit to continue to reveal truth to you from what you've read and studied.*

- *Before you start the next lesson, read 1 John 4:1—5:5. For more in-depth lesson preparation, read chapters 8 and 9, "Getting to the Bottom of Love" and "Love, Honor, and Obey," in* Be Real.

God's Love
(1 JOHN 4:1—5:5)

Before you begin …

- *Pray for the Holy Spirit to reveal truth and wisdom as you go through this lesson.*
- *Read 1 John 4:1—5:5. This lesson references chapters 8 and 9 in* Be Real. *It will be helpful for you to have your Bible and a copy of the commentary available as you work through this lesson.*

Getting Started

From the Commentary

First John 4:7–8 is the third of three expressions in John's writings that help us understand the nature of God: "God is spirit" (John 4:24 NASB); "God is light" (1 John 1:5); and "God is love." None of these is a complete revelation of God, of course, and it is wrong to separate them.

God is spirit as to His essence; He is not flesh and blood. To be sure, Jesus Christ now has a glorified body in heaven, and one day we shall have bodies like His. But being by nature spirit, God is not limited by time and space the way His creatures are.

God is light. This refers to His holy nature. In the Bible, light is a symbol of holiness, and darkness is a symbol of sin (John 3:18–21; 1 John 1:5–10). God cannot sin because He is holy. Because we have been born into His family, we have received His holy nature (1 Peter 1:14–16; 2 Peter 1:4).

God is love. This does not mean that "love is God." And the fact that two people "love each other" does not mean that their love is necessarily holy. It has accurately been said that "love does not define God, but God defines love." God is love and God is light; therefore, His love is a holy love, and His holiness is expressed in love. All that God does expresses all that God is. Even His judgments are measured out in love and mercy (Lam. 3:22–23).

—*Be Real*, pages 138–39

1. What are the practical implications of John's statement that "everyone who loves has been born of God"? How would nonbelievers respond to a statement like this? If God is love, what then is it that nonbelievers are expressing that they refer to as love? Is that still God's love?

More to Consider: First John 4:10 may be translated, "In this way is seen the true love." Define this "true love." What does false love look like?

2. Choose one verse or phrase from 1 John 4:1—5:5 that stands out to you. This could be something you're intrigued by, something that makes you uncomfortable, something that puzzles you, something that resonates with you, or just something you want to examine further. Write that here.

Going Deeper
From the Commentary

Because God is love, He must communicate—not only in words but in deeds. True love is never static or inactive. God reveals His love to mankind in many ways. He has geared all of creation to meeting men's needs. Until man's sin brought creation under bondage, man had on earth a perfect home in which to love and serve God.

God's love was revealed in the way He dealt with the nation of Israel. "The LORD did not set his love upon you, nor choose you, because ye were more in number than any people; for ye were the fewest of all people. But because the LORD loved you … hath the LORD brought you out with a mighty hand" (Deut. 7:7–8).

The greatest expression of God's love is in the death of His Son. "But God demonstrates His own love toward us, in that while we were yet sinners, Christ died for us" (Rom. 5:8 NASB)….

But the sending of Christ into the world and His death on the cross were not prompted by man's love for God. They were prompted by His love for man. The world's attitude toward God is anything but love!

Two purposes are given for Christ's death on the cross: that we might live through Him (1 John 4:9) and that He might be the propitiation for our sins (v. 10). His death was not an accident; it was an appointment. He did not die as a weak martyr, but as a mighty conqueror.

—*Be Real,* pages 140–41

3. Review 1 John 4:9–11. How is this passage similar to the most well-known verse in the Bible, John 3:16? How is it different? What unique message about love did John give his readers in these verses?

From the Commentary

At this point it would be good for us to review what John has been saying about the basic truth that "God is love."

This truth is revealed to us in the Word, but it was also revealed on the cross, where Christ died for us. "God is love" is not simply a doctrine in the Bible; it is an eternal fact clearly demonstrated at Calvary. God has said something to us, and God has done something for us.

But all this is preparation for the third great fact: God does something in us! We are not merely students reading a book, or spectators watching a deeply moving event. We are participants in the great drama of God's love!

—*Be Real,* pages 143–44

4. In what ways are God's children participants in the drama of God's love? How is God's love "made complete" in us (1 John 4:12)?

From Today's World

Christianity is the world's largest religion, claiming over two billion followers worldwide, most of those in the Western world. The cornerstone of Christianity is the death and resurrection of Jesus. And while there is much disagreement within Christianity on theological issues, most would agree that the death and resurrection of Jesus are foundational elements of the faith, both of which illustrate the great love God has for His creation. Christianity is a faith whose foundation is love. And yet Christians are often the object of derision because of the actions of individuals or groups of individuals who claim Christianity as their religion yet make statements or take actions that seem anything but loving.

5. John stated that "whoever is not from God does not listen to us." How does this truth play into the persecution or ridicule of Christianity? John warned about false prophets who have gone out into the world. Who are these false prophets today? How do they affect the way the world views Christianity? What is the best response Christians can have to false prophets? To the people whom they wrongly influence to believe Christianity isn't a loving faith?

From the Commentary

"God is love," then, is not simply a profound biblical statement. It is the basis for a believer's relationship with God and with his fellow man. Because God is love, we can love. His love is not past history; it is present reality. "Love one another" begins as a commandment (1 John 4:7), then it becomes a privilege (v. 11). But it is more than a commandment or a privilege. It is also the thrilling consequence and evidence of our abiding in Christ (v. 12). Loving one another is not something we simply ought to do; it is something we want to do.

—*Be Real,* page 148

6. What are some of the practical applications that come out of the basic truth that God is love? How does understanding God's love help Christians love others? What role does personal experience play in understanding this truth? In living it out daily?

From the Commentary

Two brand-new words came into John's vocabulary in 1 John 4:17–19: fear and torment. And this is written to believers! Is it possible that Christians can actually live in fear and torment? Yes, unfortunately, many professed believers experience both fear and torment day after day. And the reason is that they are not growing in the love of God.

The word *boldness* can mean "confidence" or "freedom of speech." It does not mean brazenness or brashness. A believer who experiences perfecting love grows in his confidence toward God. He has a reverential fear of God, not a tormenting fear. He is a son who respects his Father, not a prisoner who cringes before a judge.

We have adopted the Greek word for fear into our English vocabulary: phobia. All sorts of phobias are listed in psychology books; for instance, acrophobia—"fear of heights"—and hydrophobia—"fear of water." John was writing about krisisphobia—"fear of judgment." John has already mentioned this solemn truth in 1 John 2:28, and now he deals with it again.

—*Be Real*, pages 154–55

7. What did John mean when he wrote, "There is no fear in love" (1 John 4:18)? How does perfect love drive out fear? What are some of the fears Christians might have that need to be driven out by love?

From the Commentary

In 1 John 4:20, John wrote once again: "If a man say ..."!

We have met this important phrase several times, and each time we knew what was coming: a warning against pretending.

Fear and pretense usually go together. In fact, they were born together when the first man and woman sinned. No sooner did Adam and Eve sense their guilt than they tried to hide from God and cover their nakedness. But neither their coverings nor their excuses could shelter them from God's all-seeing eye. Adam finally had to admit, "I heard thy voice in the garden, and I was afraid" (Gen. 3:10).

—*Be Real,* page 157

8. What role does honesty play in the way we relate to God? How does honesty help us to develop confidence? How does confidence in God affect the way Christians relate toward God? Toward one another? How do we develop confidence in God?

More to Consider: Read about Ananias and Sapphira (Acts 5). What was their sin? What fears might have led them to lie? How would confidence in God have changed their actions?

From the Commentary

First John 5:1–3 speaks of joyful obedience. "His commandments are not burdensome" (1 John 5:3 NASB).

Everything in creation—except man—obeys the will of God. "Fire, and hail; snow, and vapor; stormy wind fulfilling his word" (Ps. 148:8). In the book of Jonah, you see the winds and waves, and even the fish, obeying God's commands, but the prophet persisted in disobeying. Even a plant and a little worm did what God commanded. But the prophet stubbornly wanted his own way.

Disobedience to God's will is a tragedy—but so is reluctant, grudging obedience. God does not want us to disobey Him, but neither does He want us to obey out of fear or necessity. What Paul wrote about giving also applies to living: "not grudgingly or under compulsion, for God loves a cheerful giver" (2 Cor. 9:7 NASB).

—Be Real, pages 159–60

9. What motivates us to joyful obedience? How does being part of God's family influence the reasons for our obedience? How is it possible to joyfully obey a command that will be painful or costly for us?

From the Commentary

The Greek goddess of victory was Nike, which also happens to be the name of a United States aerial missile. Both of them are named for the Greek word *nike* (NEE-kay), which simply means "victory." But what does victory have to do with maturing love?

Christians live in a real world and are beset with formidable obstacles. It is not easy to obey God. It is much easier to drift with the world, disobey Him, and "do your own thing."

But the Christian is "born of God." This means he has the divine nature within him, and it is impossible for this divine nature to disobey God. "For whatever is born of God overcomes the world" (1 John 5:4 NASB). If the old nature is in control of us, we disobey God, but if the new nature is in control, we obey God. The world appeals to the old nature (2:15–17) and tries to make God's commandments seem burdensome.

—*Be Real,* page 162

10. What does it mean to overcome the world? What gives us our victory? How easy is it to live in victory, considering all the obstacles we face in this world?

Looking Inward

Take a moment to reflect on all that you've explored thus far in this study of 1 John 4:1—5:5. Review your notes and answers and think about how each of these things matters in your life today.

Tips for Small Groups: To get the most out of this section, form pairs or trios and have group members take turns answering these questions. Be honest and as open as you can in this discussion, but most of all, be encouraging and supportive of others. Be sensitive to those who are going through particularly difficult times and don't press for people to speak if they're uncomfortable doing so.

11. What are some ways you experience God's love? How does this affect the way you show love to others? If you don't feel loved by God, how can you deal with those feelings by moving closer to God rather than further away?

12. What are some of the things you fear in life? How do those fears affect the way you live your life? How can you and God and God's family address those fears together? What would a life without fear look like?

13. Do you find obedience to God easy? Joyful? Why or why not? What are some steps you can take to discover more joy in obedience?

Going Forward

14. Think of one or two things you have learned that you'd like to work on in the coming week. Remember that this is all about quality, not quantity. It's better to work on one specific area of life and do it well than to work on many and do poorly (or to be so overwhelmed that you simply don't try).

Do you want to obey more joyfully? Do you want to be consistently loving even when your feelings of being loved go up and down? Be specific. Go back through 1 John 4:1—5:5 and put a star next to the phrase or verse that is most encouraging to you. Consider memorizing this verse.

Real-Life Application Ideas: One of John's messages in this section of his letter is confidence toward God. How can you grow your confidence? Think of some practical steps you can take this week to build your confidence—perhaps Bible study or having a conversation with a mentor or spiritual leader. Then be on the lookout for opportunities to act on that confidence as you interact with people who may not know Christ.

Seeking Help

15. Write a prayer below (or simply pray one in silence), inviting God to work on your mind and heart in those areas you've noted above. Be honest about your desires and fears.

Notes for Small Groups:

- *Look for ways to put into practice the things you wrote in the Going Forward section. Talk with other group members about your ideas and commit to being accountable to one another.*

- *During the coming week, ask the Holy Spirit to continue to reveal truth to you from what you've read and studied.*

- *Before you start the next lesson, read 1 John 5:6–21. For more in-depth lesson preparation, read chapter 10, "What Do You Know for Sure?" in* Be Real.

Certainty
(1 JOHN 5:6–21)

Before you begin ...
- *Pray for the Holy Spirit to reveal truth and wisdom as you go through this lesson.*
- *Read 1 John 5:6–21. This lesson references chapter 10 in Be Real. It will be helpful for you to have your Bible and a copy of the commentary available as you work through this lesson.*

Getting Started

From the Commentary

In 1 John 5:1–5, emphasis is placed on trusting Jesus Christ. A person who trusts Christ is born of God and is able to overcome the world. To believe that Jesus Christ is the Son of God is basic to Christian experience.

But how do we know that Jesus Christ is God? Some of His contemporaries called Him a liar and a deceiver (Matt. 27:63). Others have suggested He was a religious fanatic, a madman, or perhaps a Jewish patriot who was sincere but sadly mistaken. The people to whom John was writing were exposed to a popular false teaching that Jesus was merely a man on whom "the Christ" had come when Jesus was baptized. On the cross, "the Christ" left Jesus ("My God, my God, why hast thou forsaken me?"), and so He died like any other human being.

—*Be Real,* page 172

1. How does John's epistle refute the false teaching that claims Jesus was merely a man? Why might this have been especially important to the early church? Why is it important for Christians today?

More to Consider: Read John 15:26; 16:14. What do these verses tell us about the role of the Spirit in revealing the truth about Jesus? Why is this important for believers today?

2. Choose one verse or phrase from 1 John 5:6–21 that stands out to you. This could be something you're intrigued by, something that makes you uncomfortable, something that puzzles you, something that resonates with you, or just something you want to examine further. Write that here.

Going Deeper

From the Commentary

> How does the Spirit witness within the heart of a believer? "For you have not received a spirit of slavery leading to fear again, but you have received a spirit of adoption as sons by which we cry out, 'Abba! Father!' The Spirit Himself testifies with our spirit that we are children of God" (Rom. 8:15–16 NASB). His witness is our inner confidence that we belong to Christ—not a confidence that we "work up" for ourselves, but a confidence that God gives us.
>
> The Spirit also witnesses to us through the Word. As we read God's Word, He speaks to us and teaches us. This is not true of an unsaved man (1 Cor. 2:14); it is true only of a believer.
>
> —*Be Real,* page 173

3. Why does a Christian feel at home with God's people? What role does the Spirit play in the way we connect with other believers? How is this connection with other believers a witness to the truth that Jesus is God?

From the Commentary

> The key word in 1 John 5:6–10 is *witness*, sometimes translated "record" or "testifieth." God gave witness to His Son, but He has also given witness to His sons—to individual believers. We know that we have eternal life! Not only is there the witness of the Spirit within; but there is also the witness of the Word of God. "These things I have written to you who believe in the name of the Son of God, so that you may know that you have eternal life" (1 John 5:13 NASB).
>
> —*Be Real*, page 174

4. Read Ephesians 2:8–9. What do these verses tell us about the eternal life John referenced in 1 John 5:13? Why is it important that eternal life is a gift? How do we receive this gift (1 John 5:12; 1 Tim. 6:19)?

From the History Books

Throughout history there have been numerous Christian sects that claimed Jesus was not truly God. Some, like the Adoptionists, claimed he was "adopted" by God as His son. Others, like the Ebionites, claimed that He was merely a prophet. The Council of Nicaea declared these views heresies and they had little impact on the church in the years that followed. However, this doesn't mean the belief has completely disappeared. Outside of orthodox Christianity, there are numerous groups that are content to deny the divinity of Christ. Even among more orthodox Christians, there has been a resurgence of interest in understanding "the real Jesus," which sometimes leads to questioning His divinity.

5. What do you think prompts Christians to question Jesus' divinity? Why is the divinity of Christ so important to Christianity? How would Christianity be different if Jesus weren't God? Can someone be a God-follower and yet deny Jesus is God? Explain.

From the Commentary

God wants His children to know that they belong to Him. John was inspired by the Spirit to write his gospel to assure us that "Jesus is the Christ, the Son of God" (John

20:31). He wrote this epistle so that we may be sure that we are the children of God (1 John 5:2, 19).

—*Be Real,* page 174

6. Review the following passages: 1 John 2:29; 3:9, 14; 4:7; 5:4. In what ways are these verses "birthmarks" of God's children? What do they teach us about what it means to be children of God?

From the Commentary

It is one thing to know that Jesus is God and that we are God's children, but what about the needs and problems of daily life? Jesus helped people when He was here on earth; does He still help them? Earthly fathers take care of their children; does the heavenly Father respond when His children call on Him?

Christians have confidence in prayer, just as they have confidence as they await the judgment (1 John 2:28; 4:17). As we have seen, the word *confidence* means "freedom of speech." We can come to the Father freely and tell Him our needs.

Of course, there are conditions we must meet.

First, we must have a heart that does not condemn us (1 John 3:21–22). Unconfessed sin is a serious obstacle to answered prayer (Ps. 66:18). It is worth noting that differences between a Christian husband and his wife can hinder their prayers (1 Peter 3:1–7). If there is anything between us and any other Christian, we must settle it (Matt. 5:23–25). And unless a believer is abiding in Christ, in love and obedience, his prayers will not be answered (John 15:7).

Second, we must pray in God's will. "Thy will be done" (Matt. 6:10). "Prayer is a mighty instrument, not for getting man's will done in heaven, but for getting God's will done on earth," wrote Robert Law. George Mueller, who fed thousands of orphans with food provided in answer to prayer, said, "Prayer is not overcoming God's reluctance. It is laying hold of God's willingness."

—*Be Real,* pages 175–76

7. Where do we get our confidence in prayer? Why is it important that we can come to God in prayer for anything? Why do you think John made a point to discuss this at the end of his epistle? What potential objections or fears was he answering?

From the Commentary

> John did not write, "we shall have the requests," but, "we know that we have the requests" (1 John 5:15 NASB). The verb is present tense. We may not see the answer to a prayer immediately, but we have inner confidence that God has answered. This confidence, or faith, is "the evidence of things not seen" (Heb. 11:1). It is God witnessing to us that He has heard and answered.
>
> What breathing is to a physical man, prayer is to a spiritual man. If we do not pray, we "faint" (Luke 18:1). Prayer is not only the utterance of the lips; it is also the desire of the heart.
>
> —*Be Real,* pages 176–77

8. Why is it important to trust that God hears us when we come to Him in prayer? How does that confidence influence the kinds of things we bring to Him? What are some ways believers misinterpret what John wrote here (that "we know that we have what we asked of him")? What does praying without ceasing look like?

More to Consider: The most important thing about prayer is the will of God. How do we go about seeking the will of God through prayer? How can we differentiate between the selfish desires of our hearts and the desires God placed there?

From the Commentary

"We know that no one who is born of God sins" (1 John 5:18 NASB). "No one who is born of God practices sin" (3:9 NASB). Occasional sins are not here in view, but habitual sins, the practice of sin. Because a believer has a new nature ("God's seed," v. 9), he has new desires and appetites and is not interested in sin.

A Christian faces three enemies, all of which want to lead him into sin: the world, the flesh, and the Devil.

—*Be Real,* page 178

9. What is the "sin that leads to death" (1 John 5:16)? What is the difference between habitual sin and occasional sin? What are some ways the world, the flesh, and Satan himself tempt us to sin? How can our new nature in Christ help us turn away from these temptations?

From the Commentary

Jesus Christ is the true God. We know Him who is true, and we are in Him who is true. We have "the real thing"!

"We know that our real life is in the true One, and in His Son, Jesus Christ. This is the real God and this is real, eternal life" (1 John 5:20 PH). Reality has been the theme throughout John's letter, and now we are reminded of it again....

The Psalms contain caustic indictments of idolatry (Ps. 115:1–8; 135:15–18). To human vision, an idol looks real—eyes, ears, mouth, nose, hands, feet—but these are but useless imitations of the real thing. The eyes are blind, the ears are deaf, the mouth is silent, the hands and feet are paralyzed. But the real tragedy is that "those who make them will become like them, everyone who trusts in them" (115:8 NASB). We become like the god we worship!

—*Be Real,* pages 181–82

10. Why do you think John ended this letter with a warning against idols? How do idols keep us from God's love? From loving others? How is idol worship a path to a false reality?

Looking Inward

Take a moment to reflect on all that you've explored thus far in this study of 1 John 5:6–21. Review your notes and answers and think about how each of these things matters in your life today.

Tips for Small Groups: To get the most out of this section, form pairs or trios and have group members take turns answering these questions. Be honest and as open as you can in this discussion, but most of all, be encouraging and supportive of others. Be sensitive to those who are going through particularly difficult times and don't press for people to speak if they're uncomfortable doing so.

11. Have you ever doubted the divinity of Jesus? If so, what prompted that thinking? If you still struggle with this, what would help answer your concerns? Is it important to you that Jesus is God? Why or why not? How does that affect the way you live out your faith life?

12. How does being a child of God affect the way you see yourself? How does it affect the way you interact with God? What evidence is there in your words and actions that you belong to the one true God? If you find

it hard to feel and live in the awareness that you are God's child, why do you suppose that is?

13. What are some of the idols (things you pursue or fear more than God) you wrestle with in life? John talked about the importance of prayer just before he warned against idol worship. How can prayer help you avoid the temptations of idols?

Going Forward

14. Think of one or two things you have learned that you'd like to work on in the coming week. Remember that this is all about quality, not quantity. It's better to work on one specific area of life and do it well than to work on many and do poorly (or to be so overwhelmed that you simply don't try).

Do you want to live as a child of God? Break the temptation to worship some particular idol? Be specific. Go back through 1 John 5:6–21 and put a star next to the phrase or verse that is most encouraging to you. Consider memorizing this verse.

Real-Life Application Ideas: John's letter is all about love—God's love for His children, our love for God, our love for one another. And it's also about being honest in our relationships. Take a few minutes to think about relationships that are strained right now. Perhaps a child or spouse is upset with you. Maybe you've unintentionally hurt a coworker with your words or actions. Or maybe your relationship with God is strained because you're focused on worldly things instead of godly things. Then think about how love might be the answer to each of these strained relationships. What would it look like to love in each situation? Do that.

Seeking Help

15. Write a prayer below (or simply pray one in silence), inviting God to work on your mind and heart in those areas you've noted above. Be honest about your desires and fears.

Notes for Small Groups:

- *Look for ways to put into practice the things you wrote in the Going Forward section. Talk with other group members about your ideas and commit to being accountable to one another.*
- *During the coming week, ask the Holy Spirit to continue to reveal truth to you from what you've read and studied.*

Summary and Review

Notes for Small Groups: This session is a summary and review of this book. Because of that, it is shorter than the previous lessons. If you are using this in a small-group setting, consider combining this lesson with a time of fellowship or a shared meal.

> *Before you begin…*
> - *Pray for the Holy Spirit to reveal truth and wisdom as you go through this lesson.*
> - *Briefly review the notes you made in the previous sessions. You will refer back to previous sections throughout this bonus lesson.*

Looking Back

1. Over the past eight lessons, you've examined 1 John. What expectations did you bring to this study? In what ways were those expectations met?

2. What is the most significant personal discovery you've made from this study?

3. What surprised you most about John's emphasis on loving God and loving others?

Progress Report

4. Take a few moments to review the Going Forward sections of the previous lessons. How would you rate your progress for each of the things you chose to work on? What adjustments, if any, do you need to make to continue on the path toward spiritual maturity?

5. In what ways have you grown closer to Christ during this study? Take a moment to celebrate those things. Then think of areas where you feel you still need to grow and note those here. Make plans to revisit this study in a few weeks to review your growing faith.

Things to Pray About

6. John's letter teaches about the critical truth that Jesus is in fact God. It is a letter about the reality of God and God's love for His children. As you reflect on the words John wrote, ask God to reveal to you those truths that you most need to hear. Revisit the book often and seek the Holy Spirit's guidance to gain a better understanding of what it means to follow Christ.

7. The messages in 1 John include love for God, love for others, avoidance of worldliness, and developing confidence in your faith. Spend time praying for each of these topics.

8. Whether you've been studying this in a small group or on your own, there are many other Christians working through the very same issues you discovered when examining 1 John. Take time to pray for each of them, that God would reveal truth, that the Holy Spirit would guide you, and that each person might grow in spiritual maturity according to God's will.

A Blessing of Encouragement

Studying the Bible is one of the best ways to learn how to be more like Christ. Thanks for taking this step. In closing, let this blessing precede you and follow you into the next week while you continue to marinate in God's Word:

May God light your path to greater understanding as you review the truths found in the book of 1 John and consider how they can help you grow closer to Christ.